EXPLORING WORLD CULTURES

Thailand

Joanne Mattern

Cavendish
Square
New York

Published in 2020 by Cavendish Square Publishing, LLC
243 5th Avenue, Suite 136, New York, NY 10016

Website: cavendishsq.com

This publication represents the opinions and views of the author based on his or her personal experience, knowledge, and
research. The information in this book serves as a general guide only. The author and publisher have used their best efforts
in preparing this book and disclaim liability rising directly or indirectly from the use and application of this book.

All websites were available and accurate when this book was sent to press.

Library of Congress Cataloging-in-Publication Data

Names: Mattern, Joanne, 1963- author.
Title: Thailand / Joanne Mattern.
Description: First edition. | New York, NY : Cavendish Square Publishing,
LLC, 2020. | Series: Exploring world cultures | Includes bibliographical
references and index.
Identifiers: LCCN 2018060760 (print) | LCCN 2019001078 (ebook) | ISBN
9781502647252 (ebook) | ISBN 9781502647245 (library bound) | ISBN 9781502647221(pbk.) | ISBN 9781502647238 (6
pack)
Subjects: LCSH: Thailand--Juvenile literature.
Classification: LCC DS563.5 (ebook) | LCC DS563.5 .M28 2020 (print) | DDC
959.3--dc23
LC record available at https://lccn.loc.gov/2018060760

Editorial Director: David McNamara
Editor: Lauren Miller
Copy Editor: Nathan Heidelberger
Associate Art Director: Alan Sliwinski
Designer: Christina Shults
Production Coordinator: Karol Szymczuk
Photo Research: J8 Media

Printed in the United States of America

Contents

Introduction

Thailand is a country in Southeast Asia. Northern Thailand is connected to the main part of Asia. Southern Thailand is a long, skinny **peninsula** with beautiful beaches. The country also has mountains and forests.

About sixty-nine million people live in Thailand. Many people live in large cities. Bangkok is the capital city of Thailand. It is the largest and most crowded city in the country! Others live in the countryside.

A word that describes Thailand is "Thai." Thai people work hard. In cities, they have jobs at hotels, restaurants, and banks. In the countryside, they farm the land. Thai people also enjoy sports and music. They celebrate holidays and eat delicious foods together as a family. Children go to school and spend time with their friends.

Sports and games are important in Thailand. Religion and tradition are important too. Let's get to know more about Thailand and its people.

Bangkok's streets are crowded both day and night. Markets like this one are always bright and busy.

Thailand covers 198,117 square miles (513,121 square kilometers). In the north, Thailand shares borders with three countries. Myanmar lies to the west and north. Laos lies to the north and east. Cambodia lies to the south and east.

This map shows Thailand and its neighbors.

FACT!

Doi Inthanon is Thailand's tallest mountain. It is located near the city of Chiang Mai. It is 8,415 feet (2,565 meters) high.

A Hot, Wet Land

Thailand has a **tropical** climate. Heavy rainstorms called monsoons happen between May and October.

Southern Thailand is a long, skinny peninsula. It is surrounded by the Andaman Sea and the Gulf of Thailand. The country of Malaysia lies at the south end of the peninsula.

Traditional fishing boats on the Mekong River

The Mekong River flows along Thailand's eastern border. It separates Thailand from Laos. Many people live and work along the river. They catch fish and grow crops on farms near the water.

7

People have lived in Thailand for thousands of years. Many different groups moved there from China and other parts of Asia. A group called the Thai came about one thousand years ago.

The Thai royal family used to live in the Grand Palace. Today, it is open to visitors!

In 1511, the first Europeans came to Thailand. At first, the Thai rulers did not want the Europeans

FACT!

The first Thai kingdom was called Sukhothai. It lasted for two hundred years, from 1238 to 1438.

8

The Nation's Flag

Thailand's flag has red, white, and blue stripes. Red is a symbol of blood. White is a symbol of the Buddhist faith. Blue is a symbol of the monarchy.

Each color on the flag is important.

there. In 1851, a ruler named Rama IV welcomed Europeans. Rama IV worked to make Thailand a modern nation.

Until 1932, Thailand's kings ruled the country. Then the nation became a **constitutional monarchy**. Although today Thailand has a democratic government, the military has a lot of power.

9

VOTE ✓

The Thai **constitution** divides the government's power between three parts: executive, legislative, and judicial.

The Thai government meets in the Parliament House.

The executive part includes the king or queen and their advisors. The advisors are called the Privy Council. The king or queen signs laws and guides ceremonies. The prime minister is also

FACT!

Thailand is divided into seventy-six parts, called provinces. Each province is run by a governor.

It is against the law to say anything bad about the king or queen.

Rama X became the king of Thailand in 2016.

under the executive part. He or she is the one who leads the government.

The legislative part is known as the National Assembly. It is composed of two groups, the House of Representatives and the Senate. Together, these groups create laws. Lastly, the judicial part includes Thailand's courts. The courts make sure laws are followed. The highest court is the Supreme Court. The Supreme Court decides if laws are fair.

For most of Thailand's history, farming was the most important part of the economy. About 75 percent of all Thai people worked on farms. That began to change in

A woman works at Klong Toei market in Bangkok.

the 1960s. Today, manufacturing and service jobs are the most common.

Thailand makes many products, including electronics, cars and trucks, computers, and

FACT!

Rubies and sapphires are mined on Thailand's eastern coast.

Pretty Money

Thai money is called baht. It is very colorful and includes important people from Thai history.

Thai money comes in many colors!

clothing. Thailand sells most of these goods to other countries.

Service jobs include teachers, bankers, doctors, and government workers. **Tourism** is also important. Many Thai people work in hotels, restaurants, stores, and other businesses that help visitors.

Farming still provides some jobs. Rice is the most important crop. Thailand also grows sugarcane, coconuts, pineapples, and melons. Shrimp and other fish are also important farm products.

The Environment

Northern Thailand has low mountains and thick forests of teak and bamboo trees. Beautiful flowers like orchids grow there. East of these mountains are grassy plains.

Southern Thailand is warm and wet. Rain forests are filled with evergreen trees and mangrove trees. Elephants, tigers, and crocodiles live there.

Air pollution is a problem in Bangkok.

The Siamese fireback is Thailand's national bird. It has bright red feathers on its head and legs.

So do fruit bats, huge pythons, king cobras, and monitor lizards. These animals eat birds, rodents, and insects.

Air pollution is a problem in Thailand. It comes from cars and factories, especially in Bangkok. The government is working to improve public transportation. It is also requiring businesses to adopt more environmentally friendly practices.

Tiny Bats

Kitti's hog-nosed bat is the world's smallest bat. It is just 1 inch (2.5 centimeters) long. It lives in caves in western Thailand.

Kitti's hog-nosed bats are also called bumblebee bats.

About sixty-nine million people live in Thailand. Most of them are native Thai. Others can trace their roots back to China, Malaysia, and Myanmar.

These children live in Thailand, but they have Malay ancestry.

FACT!

Many Malays would like independence from Thailand. Beginning in 1939, the Thai government forced Malay Muslims to speak the Thai language and follow Thai culture. Independence would let the Malay people live how they want to live.

16

Hill Tribes

Several different groups live in Thailand's northern and western provinces. They are called hill tribes. Their ancestors came to Thailand from Laos, Myanmar, Tibet, and China.

Many people in Thailand have mixed ancestry. The most common mix is Thai and Chinese. In fact, Rama I, the founder of the current Thai **dynasty**, was part Chinese.

Many people in southern Thailand are Malay. The Malay people have lived on the land that is now part of the Thai peninsula for hundreds of years. They speak a different language and have different customs and traditions than most Thai people.

Lifestyle

About half of all Thai people live in the countryside. Many families live in raised houses. They are built on stilts so they do not flood during the rainy season.

It is common for traditional Thai houses to be built on stilts.

   More people have been moving to large cities like Bangkok. City dwellers usually live in small apartments. Bangkok's streets are very crowded. People ride on buses or three-wheeled cars

FACT!

Thai children usually live with their parents until they are married.

Baby Names

Many Thai names are long. Parents usually give babies a short nickname. People often use this nickname all the time.

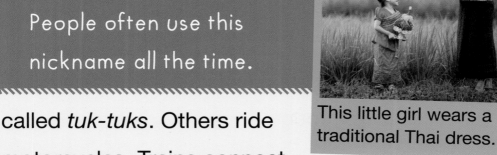

This little girl wears a traditional Thai dress.

called *tuk-tuks*. Others ride motorcycles. Trains connect cities to towns in the countryside.

Thai children must go to school from ages seven to sixteen. Many then complete three more years of upper secondary school in order to go to college. Others go to school to learn a **trade**. On average, about 50 percent of upper secondary students go to university. In the past ten years, more Thai women have gone to college than men.

Over 90 percent of Thai people are Buddhist. They follow the teachings of Buddha. He was a monk. He believed that every living thing goes through a cycle of birth, death,

Wats can be simple or fancy, like this wat in Bangkok.

and rebirth. By doing good deeds, a person can break this cycle and achieve nirvana, or freedom from suffering and desire.

A small number of Thais are Muslim. They gather in buildings called mosques for prayers.

Men in Orange

Many Thai men spend time as Buddhist monks. Monks wear orange robes. They spend time studying and doing good deeds.

Monks learn about Buddhism. They study during the day.

Every Thai village has a Buddhist temple, called a wat. Wats are in cities too. Many families have statues of Buddha at home. They place gifts like food in front of Buddha for good luck and health.

Language

Thai is the official language in Thailand. It is also the most commonly spoken language. It is a difficult language to learn. One word can

This sign at a national park is written in both Thai and English.

have different meanings. The meaning of a word changes depending on the tone of the speaker's voice. Thai has five different tones.

English is also spoken in Thailand. It is mostly used by businesspeople for work.

The National Anthem

Thailand's national anthem was written in 1932. It is called "National Song." The anthem is played on TV and radio at 8:00 every morning when the Thai flag is raised and 6:00 every evening when the flag is lowered.

The Thai alphabet was created by a king in the late 1200s. Thai has forty-four consonants and thirty-two vowels. There are no spaces between words when Thai is written down.

A small percentage of the population also speaks Burmese. This language comes from Thailand's neighbor, Myanmar.

The Thai people celebrate many Buddhist holidays. Visakha Puja, also known as Vesak, is the most important Buddhist holiday. It is celebrated in May and

New Year's celebrations are wild and wet!

honors Buddha's life. People get together in wats to sing and listen to speeches.

FACT!

The Thai king and queen's birthdays are public holidays.

Happy New Year!

The lunar new year falls in April. It is a messy holiday! People spray water and throw powder on each other for good luck.

Khao Phansa, also called Vassa, takes place from July to October. For three months, Buddhists give up things like eating meat and focus on meditation. December 10 is Constitution Day. This day celebrates when Thailand's constitution was signed in 1932.

Thai people appreciate the arts. Many pieces feature religious images. Buddha is often shown in statues, paintings, pottery, and woven silk. Music is also important. The Thai people enjoy traditional music as well as modern genres like pop and rock.

Sports are very popular in Thailand. *Muay Thai* (MOY TIE) is the national sport. It is a martial art that is a lot like kickboxing. Bands play music during matches.

Takraw (tah-KRAW) is another popular sport. It is a lot like volleyball, but players cannot use

Boxer Somluck Kamsing won Thailand's first Olympic gold medal in 1996.

FACT!

Makruk (mah-KROOK) is a popular board game. It is also called Thai chess.

26

High in the Sky

Many Thais enjoy flying kites, especially during windy days in the spring. A kite can be any shape, size, or color. Sometimes people have battles and try to knock other kites out of the sky.

their hands or arms. Many children enjoy playing *takraw*. Other popular sports are soccer, table tennis, basketball, and gymnastics.

Thailand's best Olympic sport is boxing. Boxer Somluck Kamsing was the first Thai Olympian to win a gold medal. He won at the 1996 Summer Olympics in Atlanta, Georgia.

Food

Thai food has many different flavors. It can be sour, spicy, and sweet. Spicy chilies are a common ingredient, along with many herbs and spices. Rice is part of almost every meal. Thai rice is sticky. It is often flavored with coconut milk and eaten with fish, meat, or vegetables. It is even eaten with mango for dessert.

Spicy chicken curry is a popular meal!

Satay, or grilled meat on a stick, is a popular snack in Thailand.

Street Markets

Many people shop at street markets in Thailand. These markets are filled with fresh fruits, vegetables, and

This market is split between boats and land.

meats. In Bangkok, there are even floating markets on boats!

Curry is a favorite food in Thailand. It is a stew that mixes meat, green chilies, vegetables, and coconut rice. Tea is a popular drink. Some people enjoy it with milk. Others like their tea mixed with lime juice.

Family is very important in Thailand. Meals are usually enjoyed as a family.

29

Glossary

constitution A document that outlines the laws of a country.

constitutional monarchy A system of government where a king or queen shares power with others.

dynasty A line of rulers from the same family.

peninsula Land surrounded by water on three sides.

tourism Traveling to new and interesting places.

trade A job that requires special skills and training.

tropical Hot and wet.

Find Out More

Books

Oachs, Emily Rose. *Thailand*. Minneapolis, MN:
 Bellwether Media, 2018.

Russell, Elaine. *All About Thailand: Stories, Songs,
 Crafts, and Games for Kids*. Rutland, VT:
 Tuttle Publishing, 2016.

Website

Fun Thailand Facts for Kids

https://easyscienceforkids.com/all-about-thailand/

Video

Thailand—Learn About Asian Countries for Kids

https://www.youtube.com/watch?time_
continue=6&v=m1J7AhueVGk

This video covers Thailand's culture and religion.

Index

About the Author

Joanne Mattern is the author of more than 250 books for children. She specializes in writing nonfiction and has explored many different places in her writing. Her favorite topics include history, travel, sports, biography, and animals. Mattern lives in New York State with her husband, four children, and several pets.